Yorkshire Dales Buses

West Yorkshire Road Car Company in Wharfedale

The 1950s to the 1970s

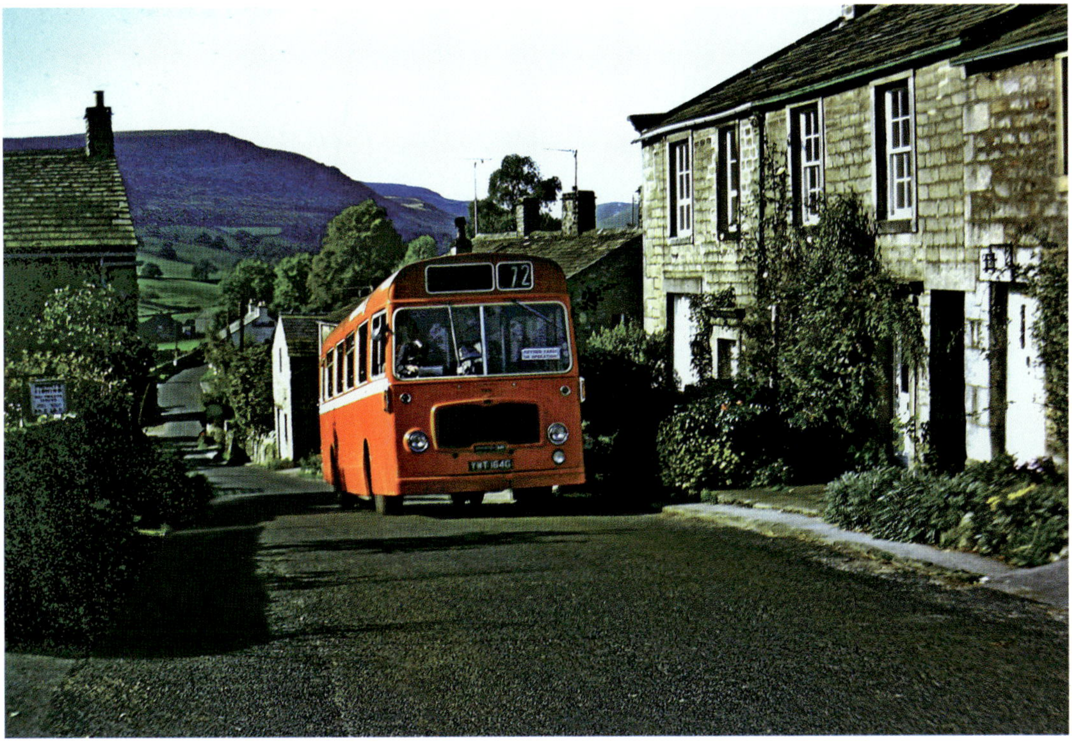

STUART EMMETT

KEY Books

BRITAIN'S BUSES SERIES, VOLUME 8

Title page image: LH1 makes its way into Appletreewick en route from Grassington to Ilkley. (Don McKeown)

Contents page image: SGL8 starts the climb up Kirkstone Pass on the Fridays-only service from Leyburn to Skipton. (SE Collection)

Published by Key Books
An imprint of Key Publishing Ltd
PO Box 100
Stamford
Lincs PE19 1XQ

www.keypublishing.com

The right of Stuart Emmett to be identified as the author of this book has been asserted in accordance with the Copyright, Designs and Patents Act 1988 Sections 77 and 78.

Copyright © Stuart Emmett, 2021

ISBN 978 1 80282 003 4

All rights reserved. Reproduction in whole or in part in any form whatsoever or by any means is strictly prohibited without the prior permission of the Publisher.

Typeset by SJmagic DESIGN SERVICES, India.

Contents

Author's Note		4
Introduction		5
Chapter 1	Starting from Skipton	11
Chapter 2	Skipton to the Dales	18
Chapter 3	Route 75 Grassington to Ilkley	77
Chapter 4	SG103 History	94
References		96

Author's Note

The West Yorkshire Road Car Company routes from Skipton and Ilkley up into Wharfedale, Wensleydale and Swaledale are some of the most scenic in the country. The variations in the buses used on these routes are also full of interest. My personal experience comes from visiting Wharfedale regularly from the mid-1950s to the mid-1960s and thereafter, on a more occasional basis, up to the mid-1970s.

I hope you enjoy the journey through this book, which has been very pleasurable to research and write and could not have happened without the many wonderful photographers who recorded history for us. Many of the images used came from the late Colin Wright who lived in Kettlewell and took some marvellous pictures. While many of his truck photographs were published between 1983 and 1987, in this book I am delighted to be able to showcase his bus photography.

Research never finishes and there are always some gaps. The same goes for some of the images where the exact location could not be fully determined, so if anyone can give clarification I will be delighted to hear from you.

My author's fee for writing this book, after deduction of costs, is going to support bus preservation and bus archives. Indeed, in company with some of the image providers, I have supplied my services free of charge to help with this initiative. All the images used, therefore, are to educate and to share nostalgia. There are a few pictures from my own collection where I have been unable to identify the photographer, for which I offer my apologies for the lack of accreditation.

Pictures/images are from the following individuals, and in no specific order: Don McKeown, Colour Classics, Omnibus Society/The Bus Archive, PM Photography and Omnicolour.

Stuart Emmett, May 2021

As we see later in the book, SGL10 got itself into trouble with the snow at Conistone in January 1962. (The Bus Archive)

Introduction

Wharfedale is within the Yorkshire Dales National Park and the River Wharfe has its source at Langstrothdale, around 1,968ft (600m) above Buckden. The River Wharfe flows through Kettlewell, Grassington, Bolton Abbey, Addingham, Ilkley, Burley-in-Wharfedale, Otley, Wetherby and Tadcaster, and travels 65 miles (104.6km) before it joins the River Ouse near Cawood, south of York.

The area known as Upper Wharfedale, which covers the river's source above Buckden to around Addingham near Ilkey, has quite a different character from the river lower down. In Upper Wharfedale the geology has limestone dominating, with grass between the many white/grey limestone outcrops, while lower down it runs in open countryside passing the edges of towns like Ilkley, Otley, and Wetherby before entering Tadcaster and the flat Vale of York. While land use in upper Wharfedale is primarily sheep farming, in lower Wharfedale it is arable with large areas of wheat, sugar beet and potatoes.

Today, tourism is significant in Upper Wharfedale and the area's traditional market town of Grassington was used for filming the 2020 TV series *All Creatures Great and Small*. Other well-known films and TV series have also used locations in Arncliffe and Kettlewell. Beside these places, this book also ventures into nearby Wensleydale, Swaledale and Nidderdale.

Bus history

West Yorkshire Road Car Company (WYRCC) had its origins back in 1898 as Harrogate Carriage Company and in 1906 became Harrogate Road Car, then Harrogate & District in December 1924, finally, becoming West Yorkshire Road Car Company from 6 December 1927.

In April 1930, routes and buses were purchased from Chapman of Grassington, the routes being five times daily from Skipton, via Grassington, to Buckden and three a day from Grassington, via Bolton Abbey, to Ilkley. These eventually became West Yorkshire Routes 71 and 75. Two occasional services to Leyburn and Hawes, in Wensleydale, were also involved and these later became Routes 78 and 79. The purchase also included the Chapman depot at the top of the Market Square in Grassington. This was built in 1922 and was used by West Yorkshire until 1957. Chapmans had a history that went back to operating horse buses, and interesting stories of this company are told by his great-grandson, Chris Binns, in his book *Old Kit Chapman* (2017).

In June 1930, West Yorkshire bought Wharfedale Motors of Skipton with 13 trips a day from Skipton to Grassington and with occasional buses from Skipton, Burnsall to Appletreewick with extensions to Litton and Skyreholme (a hamlet near Appletreewick). These became West Yorkshire routes 70, with Skyreholme incorporated into route 75.

General information

To assist in understanding some of the activities of West Yorkshire, what follows are overviews on the routes, journey times, vehicle codes and the buses used.

Wharfedale route details from 1956

Destination	Route numbers 1956 (late 1966) ((mid-1977))	Indicative number of journeys a day from Monday to Saturday	Comments
Bradford to Grassington Sanatorium	69 (0)	Sunday only in 1956, thereafter by 1960 on Sunday and Wednesday.	Finished between 1963 and 1966.
Skipton to Litton via Threshfield, Kilnsey and Arncliffe	70 (71A) ((0))	Saturday only two plus one from Grassington.	63min journey.*
Skipton to Buckden via Rylstone, Cracoe, Linton, Threshfield, Grassington, Kilnsey, Kettlewell	71 (71) ((71))	Five plus 13 to 15 shorts to Grassington.	65min journey.
Skipton locals Shortbank Road	73 (73)	23 journeys.	5mins.**
Greatwood Ave–BS–Horse Close Estate	73A (74)	Each leg every 30mins.	10mins + 10mins.
Ilkley to Grassington via Addingham, Bolton Abbey, Appletreewick, Burnsall, Threshfield	75 (72) ((772))	Four plus four shorts from Ilkley to Bolton Abbey.	65min journey. In the mid-1970s two to three return journeys ran through Grassington to Skipton.
Skipton to Tadcaster via Addingham, Ilkley, Otley, Harrogate, Wetherby, Boston Spa	76 ((784 Leeds to Skipton & 78 etc Harrogate to Tadcaster))	16 plus as an eg, 1966, shorts Ilkley to Otley, Harrogate to Wetherby, Harrogate to Boston Spa, Wetherby to Boston Spa, Wetherby to Tadcaster.	2hrs 22mins. The route was started in July 1957 and finished in April 1972.***
Ilkey to Heber's Ghyll	76A ((0))	Two on Monday to Friday and three on Saturday (1956–61).	5mins.
Ilkey to Otley	77 (not used, used 76)	Was used for around 13 shorts on route 34 Leeds to Ilkley.	20mins.
Leeds to Hawes/(Muker) ((Keld)) via Bradford, Keighley, Skipton then as 71 above to Buckden, for Cray, Aysgarth	78 (70) ((X70))	One summer only on Wednesday and Sunday with one from Skipton on Tuesday.	3hrs 53mins.****
Skipton to Leyburn as above to Buckden then via Cray, West Witton	79 (70A) ((71A))	One summer only on Friday.	2hrs 1min.

*   Litton stopped in the early 1970s and as a token replacement, a few Buckden journeys were diverted via Arncliffe.

**   Before 1958, the 73A initially ran to Horse Close Estate only. Then in 1958 Greatwood Avenue was added. Thereafter, each leg had its own timetable while the routes were interworked and used route number 73A. By 1966 they used 74, as the Harrogate to York route had now been renumbered as 84.

*** Route 76, because of space limitations this route is not covered fully in this book.

**** Route 78 notes:

- Starting on 30 July 1950, journeys commenced from Bradford to Hawes (78) on Wednesday and Sunday during the summer months. Extended to Muker over the Buttertubs in summer 1952. When buses laid over for an hour at Hawes before continuing to Muker, staying there for 55 minutes before the return to Hawes/Bradford.
- In summer 1953, it was extended back to start from Leeds.
- In summer 1977, it operated an extra 2 miles from Muker to Keld on Sundays and used route number X70 from Leeds running now via Bradford, Ilkley, Burnsall for Grassington.
- In summer 1978, it operated to Keld on Sundays and to Muker on Saturdays.
- These routes were later to be incorporated into the 'Dalesrider' series of weekend routes from West Yorkshire to the Dales.

Breakdown of some journey times

Leeds via Stanningley to Skipton	1hr 50mins
Skipton BS to Grassington	30mins*
Grassington BS to Buckden	35mins
Grassington BS to Litton	33mins
Buckden to Leyburn	56mins
Buckden to Hawes	58mins
Grassington to Bolton Abbey	45mins
Bolton Abbey to Ilkley	20mins

* 5mins longer for the few morning and evening journeys extended to/from Skipton Railway Station.

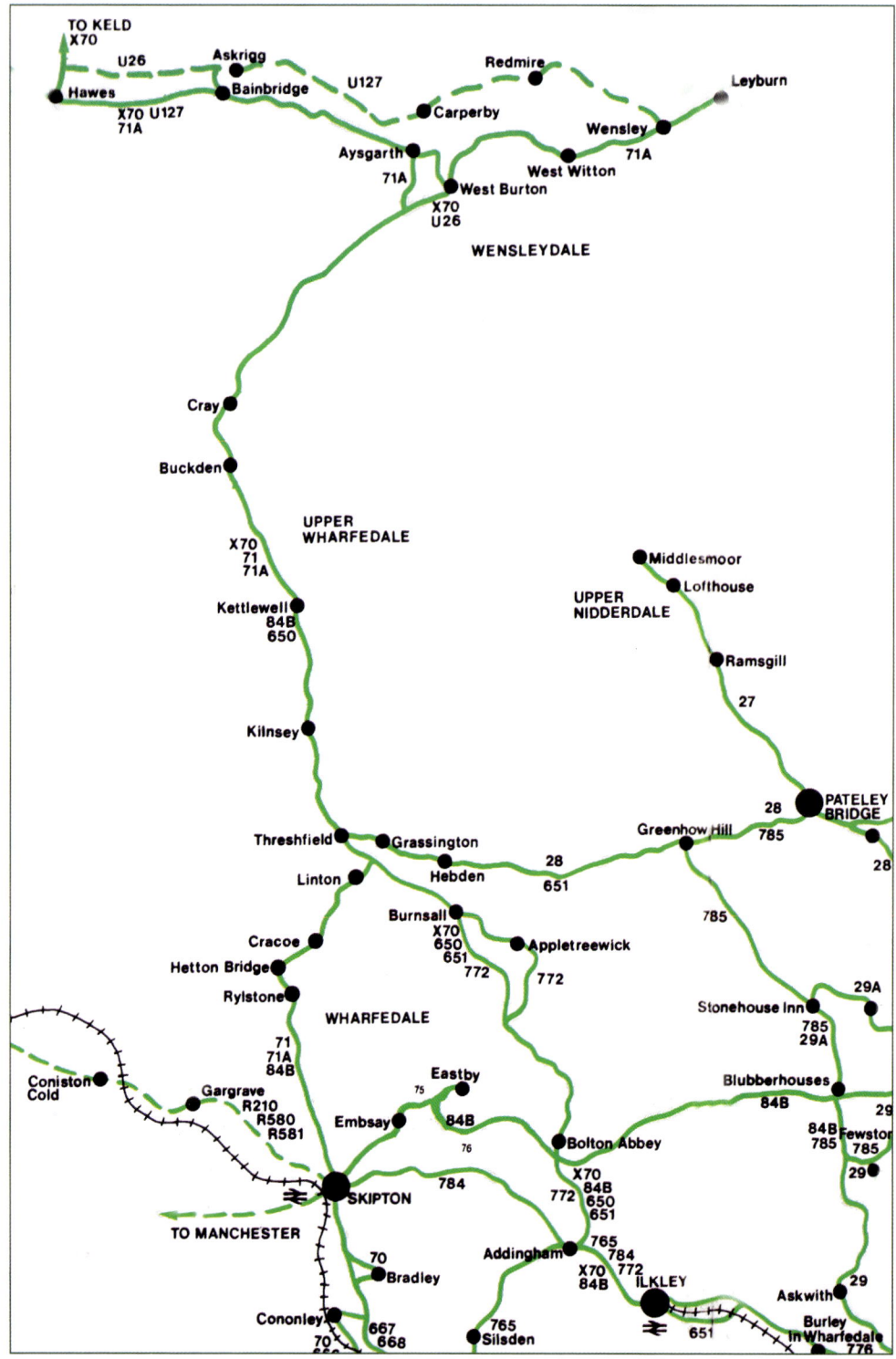

Map of the area from a 1977 timetable (by which time there had been another route renumbering, so the route numbers in the text will not fully match).

Vehicle codes

West Yorkshire had its own code system for bus fleet numbers. This is explained below in my 'A to Y' of the fleet numbering scheme that was used from April 1954 to October 1971; before this a three-number scheme was used and after 1971 it was a four-digit scheme.

Prefix: The Keighley and York fleets were prefixed 'K' or 'Y' before the standard 'WY' two- or three-letter codes.

Letter	Position	Meaning	Used in	Chassis example: Bristol unless otherwise stated
A	Third Middle	Albion engine or AEC engine	SMA DAW	SUL4A AEC Regent V
B	Second	Bristol engine	DB SB	K6B or KS6B L6B
C	First	Coach	CB	L6B
D	First	Double deck	DB	K5G
E	First	Express/dual purpose	EB	L6B
F	Second	Ford engine	CF	Ford 570E
G	Second or third	Gardner engine	DG SRG	K5G RELL6G
K	Prefix	Keighley WY	KDB	As in KDB
L	Third	30ft-long body Later was Leyland engine	SGL SML CRL	LL5G Bedford VAM14 REHL6L
LH	n/a	Bristol LH chassis	LH	LH6L
M	Second	Maximum capacity or Mid-engine or one-Man operated or Morris engine	SMG SMG SML SM	LS5G/MW5G or 6G As above Bedford VAM14 Morris-Beadle
P	Second Third	Petrol engine Perkins engine	CP/SP SMP	Bedford OB SUL6P
R	Second	Rear engine or Bristol RE chassis	SRG CRG/ERG	RELL6G or RESL6G RELH6G
S	First	Single deck	SG	L5G
U	Second	Underfloor engine	CUG SUG	LS5G or 6G or 6B LS5G
VR	n/a	Bristol VR chassis	VR	VRTSL6G
W	Third	8ft-wide body	DGW SBW	KSW6G LWL6B
X	Second	Experimental	DX	LD6B or FS6G or FS6B
Y	Prefix	York WY	YSG	Y as in YSG

Vehicles used from 1950 to the late-1970s

All were Bristol chassis with ECW bodies.

Class	Type	From	To	Comments
SG	L5G	1939 1950s	Mid-1950s 1964	Bible indicators.
EB/SB	L6B	1950s	All withdrawn by 1961	Summers only on to Hawes from Leeds/Bradford.
SBW/ SGW (rare)	LWL6B LWL5G	1950s	Mid-1960s	Mainly used summers only to Hawes from Leeds/Bradford.
SGL especially 8 to 10	LL5G	Early-1950s	1965	1950s 'workhorse' replaced by SUG/SMGs.
SG103	L5G	1959	October 1962	OMO on route 75 Grassington to Ilkley.
SUG/SMG especially from 2 to 5	LS5G	1957	1970	1960s 'workhorse' replaced by SMG MWs.
SMG especially from 25 to 31	MW6G	1963	1974	Replaced by LHs.
SMA especially 6, 13/14	SUL4A	1962	1972	Regularly on the Grassington to Ilkley route.
LH especially 1,2 and 19	LH6L	1969	Late-1970s	The 1970s 'workhorse' replaced by SRGs.
SRG especially 1372/1373	RELL6G	Late-1970s		

Bristol LS EUG/SUG/SMG class variations

West Yorkshire never bought any new LS pure service buses, although they did eventually reseat many of the dual-purpose vehicles with bus seats. In the West Yorkshire fleet, from April 1954 until 1971, the LS buses had classifications as follows:

- EUG: Express body with Under-floor Gardner engine
- SUG: Single-decker bus with Under-floor Gardner engine
- SMG: Single-decker one-Man operated bus with under-floor Gardner engine; (the 'M' has also been reported as meaning Maximum capacity)

Sixty-eight LS5Gs were received and all came new with ECW DP41F bodies. All had stepped waistbands, apart from the first (EUG1-5) and the last (EUG61-68) batches, none had rear indicators with the front indicators, being two side-by-side windows. Other operators, however, received LSs with front three-window indicators and also rear indicators.

Each of the West Yorkshire batches had slight body variations that followed the ECW practices of the day and this, along with West Yorkshire's usual policy of declassifying/reseating/livery changes resulted in many variations. This meant several changes over a vehicle's life with some buses reseated with bus seats, and then renumbered, while some others were renumbered without being reseated. Quite a complicated and variable series of events, and this was further complicated by livery changes. While all the original EUG-class deliveries were delivered in 'bus' red and cream, some later received the cream and red dual-purpose livery. Additionally, the red and cream SUG and SMG bus livery was also variably applied.

Chapter 1

Starting from Skipton

We now take a journey on the routes from Skipton and Ilkley into Wharfedale, with Grassington at the centre.

Approaching Skipton

EB8 leaving Wellington Street for a 'spirited' almost 4hr ride to Hawes. It would be downgraded to an SB8 in August 1960.

EB2 from Ilkley depot in 1960 at Skipton High Street for Pateley Bridge with a similar bus behind. From 1957 to 1962 the timetables show an unnumbered 2½hr journey from Bradford to Pateley Bridge via Keighley, Skipton, Linton, Burnsall, Appletreewick, Skyreholme lane end and Greenhow. With one return journey on Sundays in July/August as well as on Tuesdays and Thursdays on the Bradford and Keighley Annual Holiday Weeks, plus an additional journey on 'the occasion of the Nidderdale Agricultural Show'!

A former driver at the Ilkley depot, Chris Youhill, recalls that 'EB2 and 3 were at Ilkley depot when I was there in 1960–61. They had a very leisurely time Monday to Friday doing locals like the 77 to Otley, the 75 to Bolton Abbey, the 75A to Heber's Ghyll and the Semon Home specials. At weekends, though, they often came into their own on the Leeds to Keswick Express.' (The Bus Archive)

Returning to Skipton is SMG2 on a 71 and is seen roughly opposite to where EB2 is shown above and around 150m from the bus station. It was a bus long associated with these routes from 1957. In the background is a traffic roundabout that at the time took the A59 road from Merseyside via Preston and Clitheroe to York via Harrogate. (PM Photography)

Right: SUG5 with a policeman directing traffic around the roadworks. The High Street ran down to a roundabout behind SUG5 and an immediate left at that roundabout entered Newmarket Street where the West Yorkshire depot could be found. Newmarket Street continued as the A65 towards Addingham, Ilkley for Leeds, and came from Kendal via Settle. (The Bus Archive)

Below: SBW15 in July 1962 coming from the Keighley direction passes over the canal bridge and will soon be turning left into the bus station. (The Bus Archive)

SUG3 is coming into Skipton on Broughton Road, having been to the railway station directly opposite the Midland Hotel that can be seen on the right behind SUG3. Some three trips a day were extended in the morning to terminate there, with the same starting from there in the afternoon/early evening. These journeys added under 5mins to the travel time. (PM Photography)

Skipton Bus Station

While this book concentrates on the routes from Skipton in Wharfedale, Skipton was a large market town and had many interesting bus services. For example, in 1967 there was Ribble, Pennine MS and Laycock's of Barnoldswick; these have been covered in another book. The main types of West Yorkshire buses found on the Wharfedale routes are illustrated below.

SGL8 picks up on one of the Skipton local routes and was a long-used Grassington depot allocation. The local routes were effectively circular with a few spurs and were interworked with the Wharfedale routes. There were 21 SGLs in the fleet that were new in 1950–51, with Bristol LL5G chassis and ECW B39R bodies. They were mainly withdrawn in 1965–66, however KSGL20/21 waited until April 1969. SGL7 and 13 had some experimental features as will be seen later. (PM Photography)

SUG4 loads up with hikers' rucksacks. As already mentioned, this class of Bristol LS5G with (from new) ECW DP41F bodies had many body and livery changes during their lives. Introduced between 1953 and 1958, they were withdrawn between 1969 and 1971. SUG1 had some experimental features, as will be seen. (The Bus Archive)

SMG31 is waiting in the middle 'not working' area in Skipton Bus Station, while behind it can be seen a Lodekka DX-class on route 67, a Monday to Friday hourly service along the Aire Valley to Bradford and every 10mins to Keighley, journeys of 70 minutes and 38 minutes, respectively. There were 26 of these buses numbered SMG13 to 38, which were MW6Gs with ECW B45F bodies from new. They were withdrawn between 1971 and 1974 with (as will be seen) SMG33 to 38 having some late-life seating changes. (Omnibus Society)

Running alongside the River Wharfe near Kettlewell having come from Buckden, SMA6 is on a long approach to Skipton Bus Station. There were 18 of these Bristol SUL4As with ECW B36F bodies delivered new in 1962–63 and 1965, with all being retired between 1971 and 1973. There was one experimental model, SMP17, which will be seen later. (PM Photography)

KLH10 was among the large intake of LHs in 1969 (LH1 to 26) to which six were added in 1973-74 that had the BET-style rounded front. The model was designed as a small lightweight replacement for the Bristol SU chassis (the SMAs). The LH was to be succeeded in 1982 by the Leyland National B Series and some operators — for example, Cumberland Motor Services — wanted to continue ordering the LH, but orders were substituted with the Leyland National. Behind is one of the Pennines Leyland/Duple Doningtons that were used on their 'main line' service to Morecambe via Lancaster, Ingleton and Settle. (Omnibus Society)

RELL6G was new in 1970 as KSRG99 and seen here after the 1971 renumbering as 2299. With a primer-only lower front panel, it also shows the occasional use of Keighley-West Yorkshire (KWY) buses from Skipton depot. However, the Keighley-West Yorkshire title was dropped in 1974 following the local government reorganisation. Keighley Urban District Council (UDC) became part of Bradford Metropolitan District Council on 1 April 1974, and West Yorkshire reached an agreement to purchase Keighley Council's share of the joint undertaking, rather than it being transferred to the new West Yorkshire Passenger Transport Executive (PTE). Thus, the buses became part of the main fleet, losing their 'Keighley' identity and the 2xxx fleet numbers in the process, and therefore 2299 (seen here) became 1299 in March 1975. West Yorkshire bought 203 of the RELL-type between 1964 and 1974. (Omnicolour)

SRG15 leaves Harrogate for Skipton. Route 76 ran from Skipton via Ilkley, Otley, Harrogate and Wetherby to Tadcaster. It originated in the 1920s with what became Route 74 and continued past Tadcaster to York and Scarborough (around a 5hr journey). (SE Collection)

Chapter 2

Skipton to the Dales

Giving a view of the country buses from Skipton into Wharfedale, the following story was received from a former bus driver: 'Grassington received its evening papers by bus, and this continued in my time as a driver on the route. We also had a single copy to deliver to None-go-bye Farm each evening. This is on the right just after the National Park sign (just out of Skipton on the B6265), so the usual procedure was to throw the paper out of the cab window as we passed. Of course, this depended on a gap in oncoming traffic, but we must have surprised many motorists who were just far enough away to see something suddenly flying across the road from an oncoming bus!

'Additionally, a newsagent from Skipton used to drive every morning to Rylstone and Hetton Bridge and leave several newspapers in the bus shelters at these two locations for collection by their customers.'

Having left Skipton, the road is more exposed to the elements as it gradually climbs to Rylstone. Inbound to Skipton, SUG2 passes between the snow that, with the banking, is almost as high as the bus. The conductor in the door-well keeps a steady watch on the photographer. (PM Photography)

Now with better weather on this road, SUG2 makes its way towards Rylstone. (The Bus Archive)

LH1 at Rylstone from Skipton, turning left on Raikes Lane for Hetton and passing the duck pond behind the daffodils. This is around a one-mile diversion from the main B6265 road (that runs from Skipton to Grassington, Pateley Bridge to Ripon) that LH1 will later rejoin. (The Bus Archive)

Left: SUG2 heads for Hetton and passes under the railway line that formerly ran between Skipton to Grassington, but is now the freight-only line to Swinden limestone quarry. (The Bus Archive)

Below: SMG30 has left Hetton and is crossing the railway line to Swinden Quarry at Fleets Lane. It will soon rejoin the main B6265 road. (The Bus Archive)

Having left Hetton behind, SUG5 approaches Cracoe and is back on the B6265. (The Bus Archive)

Heading for Grassington and between Rylstone and Cracoe on 11 January 1959, SUG2 waits for the JCB to clear the snow. (PM Photography)

From April 1962, SUG2 became SMG2 and is seen here at Swinden squeezing past a truck beside the limestone quarry and the former Skipton to Grassington railway line that still serves this location. In railway terminology the site is known as Rylstone Quarry. There has not been a light snowfall on the wall or on the hill — it is limestone deposits from the quarry works. The whole aspect of the quarry and road changed from 1969 with the quarry set deep into the landscape. Despite some surface workings being visible from the B6265 road, the road no longer passes through the site because this is now hidden after the quarry was progressively dug down into the hill. Much of the industrial plant machinery was also moved into the quarry workings and is now concealed by the high surrounding banks of the quarry itself. Today, an underground pipeline carries limestone to the railhead. (The Bus Archive)

Products exported from the site include roadstone, agricultural lime, industrial carbonate, crushed rock aggregate and pre-cast concrete products. A significant tonnage of the quarried material is sent from the site by rail to Leeds, Dewsbury and Hull, although there are still many lorry journeys on the B6265 per year. As part of a proposal to extend the life of the quarry beyond 2030, the owners indicated a greater reliance on rail transport with a consistent reduction of lorry movements.

Right: The old way through the limestone works with SMG32, an MW6G from 1963, heading for Skipton. The white limestone dust on the roadside and elsewhere is clearly seen. (The Bus Archive)

Below: Swinden lime works in times of change when the overhead conveyors and processing plants were being demolished. LH1 passes through for Grassington. (The Bus Archive)

Left: SMG30 and other traffic on a diversion through the site during the demolition. (The Bus Archive)

Below: With the old railway bridge off the picture to the left, 1373 (which was new in 1972) makes its way on the new road past Swinden lime works. (The Bus Archive)

The year is 1955 and SUG40 is near to Swinden, joining the B6265 from Linton. Buses went via Linton village to join the B6160 road that came from Addingham, Burnsall and went on to Kettlewell, Buckden over Kidstones Pass to meet the A684 in Wensleydale. This four-minute journey via Linton would rejoin the B6265 at Threshfield and then make a short run over the River Wharfe into Grassington. The house on the corner above was the former Catch All Inn, which Swinden quarry eventually bought and closed down as the workers were spending too much time there drinking. (The Bus Archive)

SMG30 is an MW6G from 1963 and is pictured in Linton village heading for Grassington, Kettlewell and Buckden, 40mins away. (Omnicolour)

A meeting of the earlier 1951 and newer 1953 buses, with KSGL19 passing SUG5 in Linton village. (PM Photography)

SUG2 has left Linton and has joined the B6160 road from Burnsall to Threshfield. (The Bus Archive)

Left: SGW12 is seen near Threshfield and looks to be on a peak season run as it cannot show the full via/number blind. It was a rare use of this class of bus in Wharfedale, of which West Yorkshire only had 12 examples. SGW12 had been delivered in 1951 as an LWL6B (SBW) but in 1952 it was fitted with an LWL5G engine. It was withdrawn in February 1966 and scrapped.

Below: SMG27 heads into Grassington over the River Wharfe. (The Bus Archive)

Grassington

It is June 1951 and 1940-model L5Gs 202 and 204 (which became SG92 and 94 from 1954) await in Grassington Market Square for Ilkley and Skipton with two excursion coaches from Kitchin of Pudsey, near Leeds. SG92 was withdrawn in March 1956 but SG94 stayed on until September 1958 and was one of the last L5Gs to be withdrawn. (The Bus Archive)

Bristol-built 664 from 1950 was on the first West Yorkshire Information Service tour in April 1952 and is seen reversing back to the top of the Market Square in Grassington. It has been to the former Chapman garage on Hardy Grange, which was used by West Yorkshire from 1929 to 1957. No. 664 was renumbered CB5 in April 1954, became EB15 in Janaury 1959, then SB15 in August 1960, and was finally withdrawn from use in April 1962. (The Bus Archive)

The old Chapmans depot in Grassington. (R.F. Mack)

Left: The April 1952 tour also used 640, which is pictured reversing from the garage to the Market Square. New in 1939 and rebuilt by Plaxton in 1945, and again in 1952 by West Yorkshire, it was later painted red and cream before being renumbered EG7 in April 1954. The batch of six buses was withdrawn in March 1957. (The Bus Archive)

Below: SGL8 and 11 in Grassington Market Square in May 1955. Behind the Grassington Hotel in the background was Hardy Grange, the location of the former Chapman depot. The Market Square was the terminus before the new bus station and depot was opened in 1957 on Hebden Road. Complete with silver radiators, they would have been delivered black but were repainted in silver until 1956 when they were painted red; after three years it was back to black radiators, as delivered! (The Bus Archive)

Parked up at the rear entrance to the 1957 depot, 1948 EB3 shows its short-lived fleet number plate along with the extra trim on the ECW dual purpose bodies. EB3 would be 'demoted' to SB status in February 1960 and was withdrawn in June 1961. (PM Photography)

On the left is SGL13 from 1951 bound for Harrogate via Pateley Bridge on Route 28. It has the 1953 Cave Brown Cave modifications of an air scoop intake for the heating equipment over the top of the destination box, and a ventilator behind. SGL7 was similarly converted. The shorter L5G SG143 from 1950 is heading for Ilkley and at the rear is EB7 for Leeds, probably having come from Hawes. These two were retired in September 1962 and June 1961 respectively. On the left can be seen one of SUG1 to 5 that received bus seats in 1957-59 in place of their dual-purpose seats. (PM Photography)

Above: On a busy day in May 1959, SUG2 loads up with SGL12 waiting in the depot. (The Bus Archive)

Left: EUG71 and SUG4 at Grassington on Springfield Road at the side of the BS/Depot, where the MW6G EUG would have been a rare visitor. It entered service in May 1959 and was delivered in the red and cream express livery as were all the previous EUGs. Within a year, between February and May 1960, EUG71 to 75 were repainted in the cream and red livery seen left, which they retained with some interim variations until January 1969 when it was back to the red and cream, with renumbering to SUG70 to 74. They received another style of red livery with just one cream waistband, as seen on former EUG74/SUG73 later in the book. EUG71 as SUG70 was withdrawn in August 1971 and saw further service with Lincolnshire RCC. (The Bus Archive)

LH2 waits in the depot with an SMG in the shadows. (Don McKeown)

Towards Nidderdale via Grassington Sanatorium and Pateley Bridge

Laying-over for 2hrs in the Grassington Sanatorium, a 3min extension from the bus station, are SBW26, EUG/SUG37 and 38. SBW26 is on a short working to Keighley and was new in 1952, while the EUGs were new in 1955. They were renumbered as SUGs in 1959 when they retained their dual-purpose seats until withdrawn from service in September 1969 and December 1970 respectively. (PM Photography)

Just a mile beyond the Sanatorium (the chimney can be seen on the right of the horizon) is 1963 SMG14 working from Grassington to Harrogate on Route 28. Leaving a plume of diesel smoke in its wake, it is climbing out of Hebden just under 2 miles from Grassington and still has 23 miles to go. Running via Pateley Bridge in Nidderdale, where West Yorkshire had a small depot, Route 28 was normally operated by Harrogate depot and had just two journeys on Saturday with two also on Summer Sundays. (PM Photography)

It is April 1962 and SGL10 leads a posse of buses on a private hire working as they approach Stump Cross Caverns on the road between Grassington and Pateley Bridge. (The Bus Archive)

An unusual bus was used on the services from Pateley Bridge. The former EUG1 was new in 1953, but became SUG1 in 1957 after it was fitted with bus seats, and then SMG1 in April 1962. A Cave Brown Cave heating apparatus was installed in the indicator boxes, which were used for the air intake, with the destination screen now placed below the windscreen. The ventilator outtake louvre can just be seen on the roof. This equipment was installed in late 1954/early 1955 (also reported as 1956) and was retained up to the vehicle's withdrawal in July 1969.

Garaged at Pateley Bridge depot from 1956 to 1968 for the routes into Harrogate, it also regularly operated in the early 1960s, one return journey on Route 51 to/from Bradford that left Harrogate at 08.20hrs, returning at 09.40 from Bradford on Monday to Friday. Latterly, however, it returned to Harrogate at 09.25hrs on a 53. (PM Photography)

SMG26 on Pateley Bridge High Street for Harrogate. The bus depot was on the right at the bottom of the High Street. (Don McKeown)

Grassington to Kilnsey and Littondale

Pictured at Threshfield coming from Grassington, 1950 SG144 will take the Burnsall turn and then soon turn again for Linton. SG144 was withdrawn in January 1963 and scrapped. (PM Photography)

At Threshfield SMP17 turns left off the B6160 from Kettlewell and heads into Grassington on the B6265, before turning and coming back to take the same route for Skipton as SG144 above. New in 1965 as SMA17, it became SMP17 in February 1966 with its Perkins diesel engine and was reputed to be a fast machine. It was withdrawn in October 1972. (PM Photography)

On Kirk Bank above the River Wharfe, 1951 SGL14 is on the B6160 between Kilnsey and Threshfield and is near to the main entrance of Long Ashes Park holiday site. (PM Photography)

Soon to be climbing up Kirk Bank towards Threshfield, 1955 SMG42 is pictured in the River Wharfe valley after Kilnsey. With SUG39 to 45 it received bus seats in March 1964 along with its SMG coding. Here it is wearing its final livery variation before it was withdrawn from service in April 1969. (The Bus Archive)

SMG44 wears its initial SMG livery and is photographed on the same road as SMG42 pictured above. (The Bus Archive)

Above: SMG30 from 1963 heads to Kilnsey from Threshfield alongside the River Wharfe. The back road from Conistone to Grassington can be seen in the left background. (The Bus Archive)

Left: In May 1962 new SMA2 is on the B6160 towards Threshfield and has left Kilnsey. The crag can be seen in the middle background with the River Wharfe out of sight to the left of the bus. In March 1966, SMA1 to 4 (from Grassington, Skipton and Harrogate depots) became KSMAs for use on the Keighley Routes 13, 14 and 25. These buses were later withdrawn after ten years' service. (The Bus Archive)

In December 1960, SUG2 negotiates standing floodwater near Kilnsey on the way to Skipton. Heavy and persistent rain could cause rainwater run-off from fields into the road trench. (The Bus Archive)

Conistone diversion

At Kilnsey there was a variation on the Kettlewell to Grassington route. This alternative was only for a few trips a day and just for inbound journeys to Grassington, while all the other inbound journeys (basically every hour) used the B6160 main road to Threshfield and the B6265 for Grassington. Another quirk was that the Saturday only Route 70 from Litton also used the inbound Coniston variation.

SMP17 has just left Kilnsey for Skipton on the B6160 and has passed the junction for Conistone. (The Bus Archive)

Above: SUG17 approaches Conistone on a snowy day in February 1960 but will have to wait for the milk truck to move. The valley in the background looks over the River Wharfe towards Kilnsey (just visible on the right). (The Bus Archive)

Left: Conistone village with SGL10 in January 1962, which is experiencing difficulty in the snow and is receiving assistance from a local farmer and his dog. (The Bus Archive)

Above: SGL10 has given up owing to the snow in Conistone and is returning to try the main route via Threshfield. (The Bus Archive)

Right: SGL10 enters Conistone following SUG2, with the Conistone maypole noticeable on the left guarded by the railings. (PM Photography)

With Kilnsey Crag in the background, SGL10 heads through Conistone with blinds already set for its next trip from Grassington. It was actually working a 70 back to Grassington from Litton. On Saturday, a bus that went from Grassington to Litton at 07.40hrs, left Litton at 08.15 for Grassington via Conistone, and arrived at back in Grassington at 08.48. At 08.50hrs, a 75 left Grassington for Ilkley. (PM Photography)

SGL9 leaves Conistone for Grassington, having been to Litton. It is squeezing past a Leeds-registered Vauxhall Cresta E (produced from 1954 to 1957). (PM Photography)

With Kilnsey Crag in the left distance, SUG2 makes its way from Conistone to Grassington for Skipton on a wintry day. (PM Photography)

SMG32 is coming from Conistone and is near to Grassington at Grass Woods, where Bill Foster and his wife are seen moving sheep from Grassington to Conistone for North Cote farm at Kilnsey. The sheep dog keeps its eyes on the job in hand. (PM Photography)

Littondale route

On the B6160 from Kettlewell, SGL9 heads for Kilnsey and passes the junction to Arncliffe and Litton. (The Bus Archive)

Above: In Littondale, SMG46 heads from Litton towards the B6160 Kettlewell to Kilnsey road. (The Bus Archive)

Left: SMG47 returns from Litton. (PM Photography)

SUG2 nears Arncliffe with a man on a bike, a dog and two cows. (The Bus Archive)

Outside the Falcon Inn at Arncliffe, 1948 EB8 is seen in charge of a West Yorkshire Information Service tour. Arncliffe was the setting for the original *Emmerdale Farm* TV series. This then moved to Esholt village near Bradford, before a complete outdoor set was located in the grounds of Harewood House to the north of Leeds. Not to be outdone, Grassington was more recently used for the 2020 TV series of *All Creatures Great and Small*. (PM Photography)

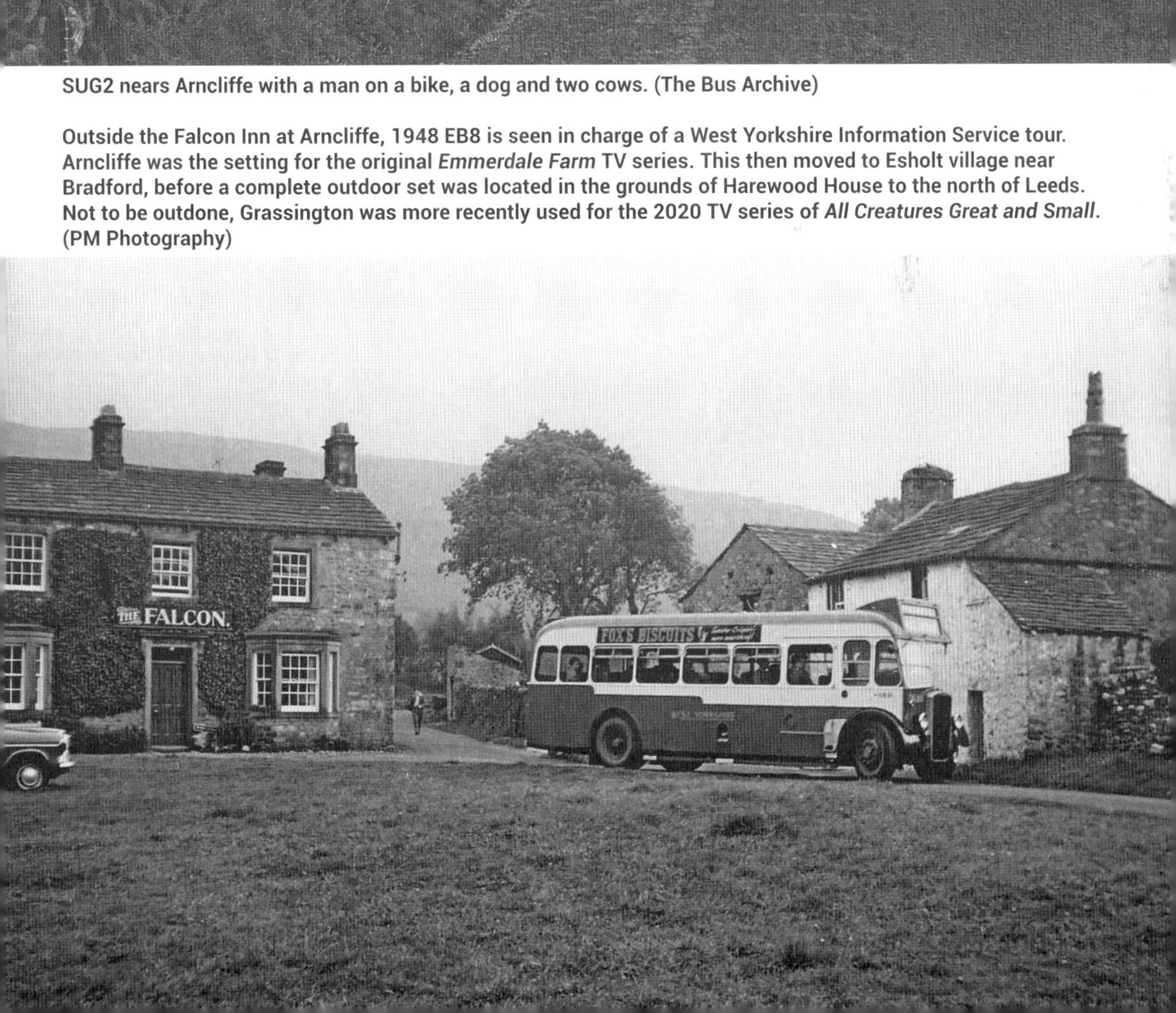

Left: SMG47 leaves Arncliffe for Litton on the 10min journey. (PM Photography)

Below: SMG47 waits in Litton on what used to be Route 70, becoming Route 71A in the mid-1960s. (PM Photography)

Kilnsey to Kettlewell

SMG25 leaves Kilnsey for Leeds with its Hawes and Muker paper stickers still in the front windscreen. (The Bus Archive)

SGL9 at Kilnsey, with the imposing overhanging crag in the background, is bound for Skipton Railway Station. This was a 3 to 5min timetabled extension beyond the bus station that had three morning drop-offs and one morning and two evening pick-ups from the railway station. (PM Photography)

SGL9 comes through Kilnsey for Buckden on the day of the Kilnsey Show, which takes place every August in the fields to the left between the road and the River Wharfe. It was first held in 1897 to promote and showcase life and farming in the Yorkshire Dales, notably the breeding of livestock, along with crafts and rural traditions. Staged in the shadow of the Kilnsey Crag, it has sheep and cattle classes supplemented by horse events with sheepdog trials attracting many top dog handlers. Towards the end of the afternoon there are the fell races, involving the punishing ascent and descent of Kilnsey Crag.

SMA1 leaves Kilnsey with a splash, heading for Kettlewell and Buckden. (The Bus Archive)

Right: KSGL19 passes Kilnsey Crag for Skipton Railway Station. (PM Photography)

Below: SUG2 seen from the top of Kilnsey Crag in April 1962. The River Wharfe is located by the tree line in the middle distance. (The Bus Archive)

Above: SMG30 from Kettlewell herds cows and is watched by the farmer as it approaches the junction for Arncliffe. The cars in the mid-background are parked off the single-track road to the hamlet of Hawkswick. (The Bus Archive)

Left: SUG2 is pictured below to the Arncliffe road junction and is about to cross the bridge over the River Skirfare that flows down Littondale, soon to join the River Wharfe. (The Bus Archive)

SUG4 continues to Kettlewell, with a view down the valley to Kilnsey Crag. (The Bus Archive)

The River Wharfe is down to the left of SGL10, around 5mins out from Kettlewell with another 5mins to go to Kilnsey. (The Bus Archive)

SUG73 still has around 2½hrs more to go to Leeds on its journey from Hawes. (The Bus Archive)

Bristol RE 1374 and sheep on the top road just outside Kettlewell with (I am reliably informed) Michael Foster who farmed at North Cote, near Kilnsey Crag, with his brother and father. For most of the year their sheep were out on the hills around Park Rash, north of Kettlewell on the narrow Coverdale Road. Here, they are being driven back to the farm, probably for shearing and fluke dosing. While 1374 waits for the sheep to finally clear the road, some have decided to vault the wall. (The Bus Archive)

SUG68, new in 1958, has just left Kettlewell, with the River Wharfe bridge visible in the mid-background. A rare bus in Wharfedale, it was among the last of the Bristol LSs operated by West Yorkshire. It was re-liveried in cream and red in 1959 to better reflect its dual-purpose seating. In 1963 it became SUG68 with a cream and red scheme livery as seen above, and then finally it received an overall red livery with just a cream waistband. SUG68 was withdrawn in 1971.

This batch (EUG61 to 68) had a distinctive Cave Brown Cave radiator below the windscreen and the body no longer featured the stepped waistband. However, the cream lower waistband was further down and deeper than on EUG 1 to 5 and was also continued below the windscreen.

These were some of the last LSs produced and interestingly, earlier in November 1957, the next registration TWT122 had gone to EUG70. This was the Bristol replacement for the LS with ECW DP41F body and was one of seven pre-production MWs (the others were three buses, two coaches plus an incomplete bus for development purposes by Bristol). (The Bus Archive)

With a fine view up the valley towards Buckden, 1969 LH2 leaves Kettlewell. The location was used as the fictitious village of Knapely during filming in the summer of 2002 of the *Calendar Girls*, based on the true story of how Rylstone Women's Institute produced a nude calendar to raise money for leukaemia research. (The Bus Archive)

Kettlewell with a West Yorkshire MW bus (SMG class) making its way out of Kettlewell over the River Wharfe on Route 71 to Skipton, some 14 miles (22.5km) away. It will go via Grassington and continue south to Skipton, which is close to the River Aire. Meanwhile, the River Wharfe after Grassington flows south-easterly via Burnsall and Ilkley. (PM Photography)

LH 1179 from 1974 allows two identical sisters to leave Kettlewell, with the surrounding limestone hills seen clearly in the background. (The Bus Archive)

CBW10 is pictured in Kettlewell, parked near the River Wharfe bridge. In April 1962 it was downgraded to SBW10 and missed out on the interim EBW classification applied in 1960 to the former CBW1 to 9. Seen shortly after being renumbered in July 1962 along with an EUG MW type, both vehicles are parked just before the small bridge over Kettlewell Beck that is directly behind the EUG. SBW10 was withdrawn September 1963. (The author is pleased to see it here, as in his youth this was the only bus in the fleet that he never actually saw.) (The Bus Archive)

Making its way into Kettlewell for Hawes on the B6160, 1948 EB5 is lining up to turn right to run the loop around the village; going left would take it over the small bridge. The B6160 road down into Kettlewell from Skipton can be seen on the hill to the left. EB5 was renumbered SB5 in August 1960 and was then withdrawn in September 1961. (The Bus Archive)

Photographed in July 1961 with the bridge to the left of the picture, SB10 and what appears to be SG106 have run around the loop in Kettlewell and are about to rejoin the B6160 for Skipton. (The Bus Archive)

SMG47 has just left the B6160 and loops its way round Kettlewell, soon to turn left towards the Green and the King's Head pub. (The Bus Archive)

In April 1962, SUG5 is heading for Skipton and is seen outside the King's Head pub in Kettlewell. (The Bus Archive)

SUG2 from Skipton is on the loop in Kettlewell. The tractor has moved over into the King's Head pub car park to allow SUG2 to swing out so it can turn left just past the pub (out of view on the right). Notice what looks like an army Austin Champ jeep and an Austin A40 Somerset car behind SUG2. (PM Photography)

Above: SBW28 is just up from the King's Head and is offloading before continuing for Hawes. From 1963 to 1966 West Yorkshire had a programme to fit reduced front indicators and, with single-deckers, to remove them completely at the rear. Fortunately, SBW28 has had a 'tidy' treatment as some were merely painted over, leaving a T-shape for the destination and route number. (The Bus Archive)

Right: EB7 passes the post office on the loop round Kettlewell and will soon turn left into Middle Lane. (PM Photography)

SMP17 leaves Middle Lane on its way to Skipton. The square shading on the front grill was exactly where the distinctive Perkins badge/logo had been applied for publicity purposes following the fitting of the Perkins engine. This bus was considered a 'flyer' to crews. (The Bus Archive)

SGL8 in January 1962 has turned the corner into Middle Lane and is unloading, with one hardy lad wearing shorts! One wonders if they have packed their crampons for their likely walk to the campsite. (The Bus Archive)

SMA1 waits at the end of Middle Lane outside the Bluebell Hotel and is being inspected by a dog. The bridge taking the main B6160 road is behind the bus stop and the Ribble touring coach. (The Bus Archive)

Right: With the Bluebell Hotel in the background, EB5 pulls away from Kettlewell for Hawes. (The Bus Archive)

Below: SMG28 leads off from Kettlewell, leaving a smoking SMG27. The 71 Buckden service was timed to leave at 12.30hrs, while the 70 for Hawes was due to leave at 12.35. The Hawes bus had left Skipton at 11.25 with the Buckden bus at 11.35hrs. However, the Hawes bus has laid over for 16 minutes in Grassington and the Buckden bus left 5mins before the Hawes bus was scheduled to leave. Grassington was probably a convenient comfort break on the long journey from Leeds, but no such timetabled break existed for the return journey. (The Bus Archive)

SUG4 arrives in Kettlewell from Buckden with one expectant passenger already on the move. (The Bus Archive)

Kettlewell to Buckden

SUG2 heads out of Kettlewell towards Starbotton for Buckden with the River Wharfe over the wall on the right. (PM Photography)

Passing Kettlewell Primary School on the Buckden road in July 1962 is SBW27 (in the batch SBW13 to 35, 1 to 12 were the CBW class). A duplicate SG or SGL follows behind. (The Bus Archive)

At Starbotton, with the Fox and Hounds pub on the right, which is about halfway between Kettlewell and Buckden, SBW19 (new in 1952) on the 78 to Hawes and SUG2 from 1953 have come down the valley for Skipton. Both buses were eventually withdrawn after 16 years' service.

Heading for Leeds from Hawes is SUG73, pictured at Starbotton. New as EUG74 in 1959 (in the batch EUG71 to 75) and delivered in a red and cream livery, these vehicles were repainted cream and red in 1960. On being renumbered SUG70 to 74 in 1969, they reverted to red and cream, as seen here. However, this was a slightly different variation on the red and cream from when they were delivered. Withdrawn in 1971, three of this batch went to Lincolnshire RCC and were reseated from DP41F to B43F. (The Bus Archive)

Above: Heading for Kettlewell, SMG28 leaves Starbotton on the Friday Leyburn to Skipton route. (The Bus Archive)

Left: SUG2 and SB7 photographed in July 1961 on the B6160 between Starbotton and Buckden. (The Bus Archive)

On a wintry day with snow still clinging to the telephone wires and sheep sheltering at the side of the barn, SMG30 (complete with conductor) has left Buckden in the background and heads down towards Starbotton. (The Bus Archive)

SMG2 viewed in May 1963 after being renumbered in April 1962. It is nearly at Buckden and the crew have already reset the blind for the return to Skipton. (Colour Classics)

SG139 as 260 (and therefore pre-1954) in Buckden heading for Hawes with the conductor climbing back on board. Note the sack in the well behind the nearside front wing, which suggests there was probably no rear boot or space on this full-looking bus. (Omnibus Society)

SGL13 lays over in the sunshine outside the Buck Inn at Buckden in the late 1950s, judging by the cars. (PM Photography)

A snowy Buckden pictured in January 1962 with SGL8. The road behind SGL8 is via Cray and Kidstones Pass into Wensleydale, which was used by the Hawes and Leyburn routes. The road to the left for Hubberholme and Hawes is a narrow single-track road and was not used by the stage buses. It passes close to the source of the River Wharfe and when 'on the other side' at Hawes in Wensleydale it passes Gayle, the home of a small depot for United AS of Darlington. (The Bus Archive)

Right: SMG30 is turning around just past the Buck Inn and looks to have suffered damage to the rear panel, which is not surprising given the challenging conditions. (The Bus Archive)

Below: SUG5 leaves from the Buck Inn for Skipton. (The Bus Archive)

Buckden to Hawes and Leyburn in Wensleydale

On 'the tops' above Buckden and past Cray, SMG31 heads towards Hawes and Kidstones Pass in August 1966. (The Bus Archive)

One of the few RESLs with West Yorkshire, 1106 from 1972 on the X70 is returning to Leeds on 'the tops' after climbing up Kidstones Pass from Wensleydale. Delivered to York as 3106 in the batch 3104 to 3107, these RESLs passed to Keighley and then finally to the main fleet in 1975. (Omnibus Society)

It is May 1964 and 1952 SBW31 is seen here nicely steaming up Kidstones Pass on its way back from Hawes to Bradford. On the left is a derelict horse-powered snow plough. (The Bus Archive)

EB9 climbs the Kidstones Pass on its way back to Leeds. The gradient varies from 1 in 12 to 1 in 6 on the steep climb to the 1,463ft (446m) summit. (PM Photography)

SMG25 climbs Kidstones Pass in August 1966 with the usual following posse of cars. (The Bus Archive)

From Aysgarth in Wensleydale the road is narrow towards Kidstones Pass. SMG30 (now 1138 from October 1971) meets an Ellen Smith coach. (Don McKeown)

The road into Hawes

Wensleydale on a Tuesday in August 1966, with SMG16 leaving Bainbridge from Hawes and heading for Skipton. (The Bus Archive)

SMG29 passes over the crossroads on the A684 at Bainbridge, with four more miles to go to Hawes. (The Bus Archive)

SMG31 passes the boundary sign for Hawes, while a couple have parked their Morris 1100 and are using the bench on the left to watch the world go by. (The Bus Archive)

SMG28 enters Hawes on the one-way road system that encircles the town centre. (The Bus Archive)

SGL9 is in Hawes on the summertime service with a layover of about 3½hrs before its return to Skipton (Tuesday), or onwards to Bradford/Leeds (on Saturday/Sunday). Also seen on the left is a Ribble Burlingham Seagull on an excursion, a UAS LS on what may be Route 127 and a UAS L approaching on Route 26. The 127 used to run from Ripon, Masham, Leyburn, Wensley, Redmire, Askrigg, Bainbridge to Hawes and Garsdale (for the Settle to Carlisle railway), while the 26 ran from Darlington to Richmond, Leyburn, Wensley, West Witton, Aysgarth, Bainbridge and Hawes. Between Leyburn and Hawes, the 127 ran on the north side of the River Ure and the 26 on the south.

SBW20 lays over in Hawes during August 1963 with a bent lifeguard rail, which may have been damaged on this journey from Leeds. (Roger Holmes/The Bus Archive)

EUG85 is seen in Hawes and was one of the 1961 batch EUG81 to 89, most of which had this smaller CBC front intake. They were also the only EUGs to be delivered in cream and red, but this was a different application from that seen above. Between December 1969 and October 1971, they were also re-engined to MW6G and the EUG's MW5G engines were reused in the donor batch of withdrawn former CUG LS6G coaches. The CUGs were said not to have been operated in service with West Yorkshire with a replacement 5-cylinder engine.

In 1969, EUG85 had become cream and red in the style seen above, then, in 1970, 81 and 82 became red buses as SUG80 and 81. By the time of the October 1971 renumbering scheme, they reverted to cream and red, again in the style above. For the 1973 season some buses were painted into the 50/50 NBC semi-coach red and white livery, however, withdrawal had started and three went to Lincolnshire RCC in early 1973. The last of the batch was withdrawn in 1975. (The Bus Archive)

From Hawes to Muker and Keld in Swaledale

EUG85 heads from Hawes for Muker via Buttertubs Pass on the 30min extension from Hawes. (The Bus Archive)

August 1966 with SMG25 coming from Swaledale in Buttertubs Pass and heading for the top and then down into Hawes. (The Bus Archive)

Above: An NBC-liveried SMG with DP seats pauses on Buttertubs. The last six MW6G buses, SMG33 to 38, which were new in 1964, received these seats in 1971 from withdrawn former EUG MW5Gs. Bus seats from the SMGs were fitted into former dual-purpose EUGs that were sold to Lincolnshire RCC. (Don McKeown)

Left: LH1177, new in 1973, pauses on the way down from Buttertubs Pass. (Don McKeown)

Swaledale with SMG25 waiting in Muker in August 1966. Later, the route terminated in Keld, just over 2 miles to the north and a timetabled extra 10mins from Hawes. (The Bus Archive)

The road to Leyburn

SMG31 negotiates a tight bend at Thoralby as it heads for Leyburn in September 1969. (The Bus Archive)

Left: SMG31 again, this time at West Witton in September 1969 with 4 miles to go to Leyburn. (The Bus Archive)

Below: Despite the destination showing on its blind, SGL8 is in Leyburn marketplace and is ready with a good load for its summertime Fridays-only run back to Skipton. It had a long layover in Leyburn when, after arriving at 11.00hrs, it did not depart again until 14.45, almost 4hrs later, the journey time from Skipton was just under 2hrs. (Omnicolour)

Wensleydale was United territory as these four MWs at Leyburn illustrate. The 72 (formerly the 20 up until 1968) ran from Darlington to Northallerton, Bedale into Leyburn; the 26 from Darlington to Richmond, Leyburn, Wensley, West Witton, Aysgarth, Bainbridge to Hawes; and the 127 from Ripon, Masham, Leyburn, Redmire to Hawes.

Chapter 3

Route 75 Grassington to Ilkley

The route from Grassington to Ilkey came with the Chapman buyout in 1930 and has been well described by former West Yorkshire conductor and driver, Chris Youhill: 'It was a lovely route, but roadwise dreadful with dry stone walls, no kerbs or verges, Bolton Abbey arch, Barden bridge, and hordes of motorists and others towing large caravans – many such drivers seemingly with not the vaguest idea of the dimensions of their vehicles. The famous West Yorkshire Bristol L/ECW saloon SG103, converted by the company to forward entrance OPO, was the basic performer on the full-length weekday journeys on the route for many years.'

SG103 was a unique Bristol L in the fleet with its front entrance and worked the 75 from March 1959 until October 1962 when a Bristol SUL (coded SMA) replaced it.

In the summer months on weekdays the 75 was run from Grassington depot with one bus. A typical timetable reveals how the day started with a short to Bolton Abbey at 07.15hrs and back at Grassington at 09.00. Then the route was fully covered down to Ilkley, arriving at 10.05, leaving at 10.55 and back into Grassington at 12.00hrs. Another three trips would follow, leaving Grassington at 13.00hrs, 16.00 and 18.35hrs, with returns from Ilkley at 14.10, 17.30 and 20.00hrs. The bus finally arrived back at the depot at 21.05hrs for close of the day.

Ilkley depot meanwhile would run shorts to Bolton Abbey, leaving Ilkley at 12.10hrs and 19.00 for a 40min round trip, also providing the occasional duplicate to Addingham which was 10mins away.

With passengers expecting the crew's arrival, 1940 SG91 sits in Grassington waiting for the driver. Is he approaching from behind and is on his way? This is one of the author's favourite pictures because of the lady standing waiting with her handbag. He is sure he's seen her before in other pictures! SG91 was withdrawn in May 1955 after being renumbered from 201 in April 1954, thus neatly dating this picture between these years. (PM Photography)

SUG/SMG2 and SMA1 at Grassington with the SMA bound for Skyreholme, a short diversion off the route past Appletreewick. The SMA was new in 1962 and became a KSMA in 1966, so this dates the photograph between 1962 and 1966, and before the route was renumbered 72 in around 1966. SMG2 was withdrawn in 1969 and SMA2 in 1972, with service lives of 16 and 10 years, respectively. (PM Photography)

SMA14 has run for 5mins from Grassington via Threshfield and passes under the old railway bridge at Great Bank Top. This had carried the former railway line from Skipton to Grassington, the line now being freight only to Swinden limestone quarry. SMA14 has 10mins more to go to Burnsall for Ilkley. (The Bus Archive)

Right: Heading towards Linton crossroads for Burnsall, SMA14 is pictured with Great Bank Top in the background. (Don McKeown)

Below: SMA14 is at Linton crossroads on a 2-mile journey down into Burnsall for Ilkley on the B6160. (The Bus Archive)

SG103 is a mile or so outside Burnsall heading for Grassington and with 1/8th of a mile to go for Thorpe Lane. The hill behind with trees on it is Simon Seat, near Skyreholme. SG103 is bearing slightly left and then has a hard right on the steepest part of the hill, followed by another left to the summit and Thorpe Lane. (Omnibus Society)

Having just left from behind the River Wharfe in Burnsall village, SG103 is heading for Grassington where it will cross the Wharfe again. (PM Photography)

SMA15 has just crossed the River Wharfe at Burnsall from Barden Towers, on the back road via Appletreewick. With the Red Lion Hotel on its right-hand side, SMA15 has just 15mins to go to Grassington, some 50 minutes after it had left Ilkley. (Omnicolour)

This photograph of SMG25 showcases a rare use of this class of bus on the route. It is pictured as it passes the Red Lion in Burnsall and leaves the B6160 for the back roads to Barden Bridge via Appletreewick. (The Bus Archive)

SMA14 climbs away from Burnsall up to the junction for Harlington for Hebden on the B6265 Grassington to Pateley Bridge road. It has a 10min journey to Appletreewick and will run down the Wharfe valley all the way into Ilkley. (The Bus Archive)

Passing the junction to Harlington and Hebden, SGL10 has a few minutes to go to Burnsall. (PM Photography)

Right: Despite the destination on the screen, SMA15 is bound for Ilkley and is approaching Appletreewick from Burnsall. (Don McKeown)

Below: LH1 passes through Appletreewick bound for Ilkley. (Don McKeown)

Skyreholme short working

Operating the Saturday-only one return working to Skyreholme, SGL12 is parked with no driver on the mile-long cul-de-sac for buses from the Appletreewick/Barden road. The vehicle is actually coming away from Skyreholme and joining the Appletreewick/Barden road at its junction for the road to Greenhow and Pateley Bridge. (PM Photography)

KSMA4 is seen on 17 June 1967 in Skyreholme heading past the cotton and calico mill to turn around. (The Bus Archive)

Above: At Sykreholme, KSMA4 is now turning around by reversing up the no-through road. (The Bus Archive)

Right: An SMA waits by the cotton and calico mill at Skyreholme ready for the return journey to Grassington. It left Grassington at 21.15hrs for its 30min journey and returned at 21.45. The route was not in the June 1968 timetable. (The Bus Archive)

Barden to Ilkley

The section of road from Burnsall and Appletreewick is on a narrow stretch above the River Wharfe. At Barden Bridge the carriageway drops down to cross over the River Wharfe once more. The narrow bridge has a 90° turn from the Appletreewick direction and is pictured with SG103 squeezing over from Ilkley and about to take the tight bend. (PM Photography)

SMA6 is en route to Ilkley and having crossed over Barden Bridge in the valley bottom it makes its way up to Barden Towers. There it will rejoin the B6160 main road that runs down from Burnsall to Addingham. (Omnicolour)

Coming from Ilkley and heading on the back road for Barden Bridge and Appletreewick, SGL11 is on the junction at Barden with the B6160 from Burnsall to Bolton Abbey and Addingham. It is equipped with snow chains, which is a first sighting for the author of such being used on a bus. (PM Photography)

On the B6160 just down from the junction with the road to Appletreewick, SMA1 picks up a passenger outside Barden Tower. This historic building was used as a hunting lodge in the 15th and 16th centuries before falling into disrepair in the 18th century. It is now part of the Bolton Abbey Estate and is listed as a medieval fortified tower. (The Bus Archive)

Crossing the river bridge, 1939 SG21 is between Barden Tower and close to the Strid car park. The River Wharfe narrows at a point called the Strid, near Bolton Abbey, where there is a deadly combination of fast currents and underwater rocks. SG21 was withdrawn in August 1955. (PM Photography)

SMA14 passes under Bolton Abbey arch with the remains of the abbey away to the right behind the wall, where the land runs down to the River Wharfe. (Don McKeown)

SMA14 is on its way back to Grassington through the abbey arch. (Don McKeown)

SBW15 has turned at Bolton Abbey on a short working from Ilkley. (PM Photography)

SMA14 passes though Bolton Abbey village, close to where SBW15 is seen in the photograph on the previous page. (Don McKeown)

Ribble 673 at Bolton Abbey returns to Skipton on the lanes through Halton East and Embsay, which was a 26min journey. The route passed to West Yorkshire when Ribble closed its Skipton depot in May 1975, and West Yorkshire then took over the Ribble Skipton services to Bolton Abbey and Easby. Later, West Yorkshire closed its Skipton depot in August 1983 and the former Ribble routes, along with the West Yorkshire Skipton local routes, all passed over to Pennine Motor Services until 1994. (Don McKeown)

SMG18 is pictured beyond Bolton Abbey and has turned off the A59 main road heading for Addingham on the B6160 for Ilkley. (PM Photography)

SG103 passes the Crown Hotel at Addingham at the end of the B6160 and joins the main A65 Skipton to Ilkley road (this road was also covered by Route 76 from Skipton to Tadcaster). (WYIS)

Johnson's café provides the backdrop for 1939 SG21 as it heads into Ilkley centre from the A65, with a Jowett Bradford van turning left. It will proceed up Brook Street for Station Road and then turn around to come back on to Brook Street for its next journey.

On a short from Bolton Abbey, EB3 emerges from West Street into Brook Street. This saved using the traffic light junction behind, where the double decker (a DX) is headed for on a 76 for Skipton. EB3 will soon run under the railway bridge and offload. (The Bus Archive)

SGL11 has arrived in Ilkley from Grassington under the imposing railway bridge (demolished in 1966) on Brook Street that linked the town with Skipton. The conductress is dealing with the waiting passengers and a lad with a basket looks to be on a delivery (Dewhurst's the butcher was nearby). Behind is a Bristol K double-decker of Keighley West Yorkshire on Route 12, a 55min journey from Ilkley to Haworth, which ran out to Addingham on the A65 then over 'the tops' into Steeton in Airedale for Keighley, and finally, to Haworth in Bronte country. (PM Photography)

Ilkley had many bus connections and, as seen here, KDX40 when it was at Ilkley depot has run in on Route 63 from Bradford. Normally, KDX40 would be used on the Keighley Route 12 (as with the Bristol K in the picture above). (PM Photography)

Chapter 4
SG103 History

New into service at Harrogate on 1 January 1947 with fleet number 208, this vehicle became SG103 in April 1954. It was due for an overhaul in October 1955 when it received a front entrance for one-man operation, making it unique for West Yorkshire at that time. The rear entrance was bolted up and the front nearside panel removed to permit installation of an electrically operated jack knife door, as used on the LS5Gs/SUG class. It benefitted from a completely rebuilt front bulkhead with the offside half removed and an arch fitted to allow driver entry. The original driver's door was bolted up and the four front seats were removed, with an arm placed in the centre of the rear seat, which resulted in making the vehicle B30F. Replacing the original standard square-type sliding windows with full windows throughout, ventilation was also provided using Beadle-Tilling-type adjustable screw vents. Although the rear indicator was retained, it was painted out.

SG103 re-entered service at Harrogate on 10 February 1956 and its initial duties as a one-man operation (OMO) bus – the first one for West Yorkshire – was on the short 10min local service from Harrogate to Cornwall Road (7). SG103 remained at Harrogate for three years.

SG103 is seen here on Route 7 in Harrogate.

On 25 March 1959, SG103 was transferred to Grassington from where it started OMO on Route 75. Its place on the Cornwall Road service was taken by SUG34, being one of a small number of LS5Gs that had been adapted for OMO. SUG19, 23 and 24 were the others. It was initially planned to convert Route 75 to OMO with a SUG, but it was pointed out that Barden Bridge could be a difficult obstacle for this size of vehicle. SG103 continued to work from Grassington for the rest of its service life and was withdrawn on 31 October 1962, to be replaced by an SMA.

SG103 at Middlesmoor in Nidderdale on a West Yorkshire Information Service (WYIS) enthusiasts' tour in September 1957. (The Bus Archive)

References

Binns, Christopher, *Old Kit Chapman*, self-published (2017) (old.kit.chapman@gmail.com)

Emmett, Stuart, *Skipton 1967, with Pennine, Laycock, Ribble and West Yorkshire Buses*, Stenlake Publishing (2020)

Jenkinson, Keith, *West Yorkshire: A National Bus Company*, The Transport Publishing Company (1977)

Jenkinson, Keith, *Northern Rose: The History of West Yorkshire Road Car Company*, Autobus Review (1987)

Anon, *The West Yorkshire Road Car Company Limited, Fleet History PB12 Part 2*, The PSV Circle, the Omnibus Society and West Yorkshire Information Service